# Bobbin Lacemaking
## for Beginners

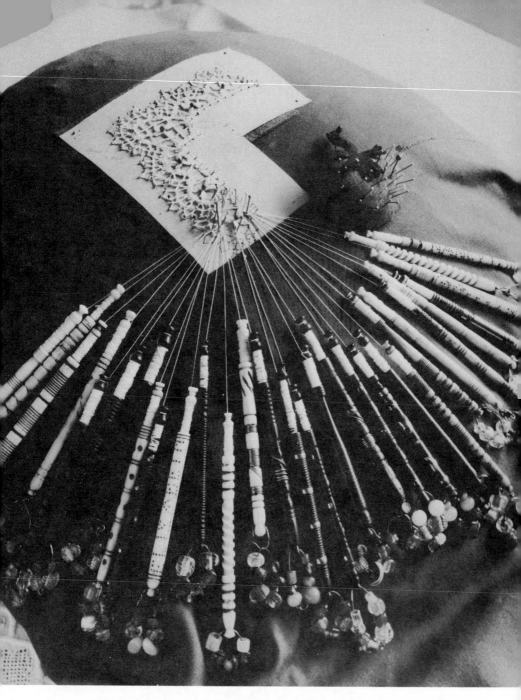

*A complete picture of bobbin lacemaking. A beautiful array of traditional bobbins, wound with thread and arrayed on the cushion during the making of a traditional Bedford handkerchief.*

# Bobbin Lacemaking for Beginners

## Amy Dawson

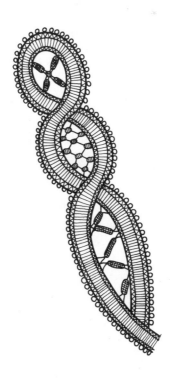

**Blandford Press**
**Poole    Dorset**

First published in the U.K. 1977 by Blandford Press,
Link House, West Street
Poole, Dorset BH15 1LL

Reprinted 1978
Reprinted 1982

ISBN 0 7137 0817 4

Printed in Great Britain by Unwin Brothers Limited
The Gresham Press, Old Woking, Surrey

# Contents

# Acknowledgements

All of the lace illustrated in the book is the work of the author. The photographs of the displayed finished articles were taken by Mike Weaver and the display on page 84 by Nicholas Cave Ltd.

The instructional line illustrations which accompany the sample patterns were prepared by Rodney Paull from the author's original drawings.

# Preface

It is often said that nothing is too difficult to achieve if you are shown 'how' to do it.

Many competent embroiderers, knitters, and crochet workers will find lacemaking easy to accomplish, if they have time and the desire to learn this ancient and rewarding craft.

Ideally, to take lessons and be taught how to make lace is the best possible way to achievement. As there are few teachers to be found nowadays, I hope this book will be of practical help to those who have 'time and the desire to learn'.

Many books have been written on the history of lacemaking, from Biblical times to the present day. From 1685, when the Huguenots, fleeing from religious persecution, settled in the West and Midlands of England, and taught the women of the two areas to make lace, it was estimated that 100,000 workers earned a living from this craft.

Many schools in Belgium, France and Italy taught lacemaking to the very young, and hand-made lace was much sought after by the Church, royalty, and very rich gentle-folk.

In France, special lace schools were opened at Le Puy, and Château Lauray at Alençon, employing 30 teachers from Venice, and 200 from Flanders. To employ these children, factories were opened elsewhere in France, and so a lace industry flourished, supplying King Louis and his courtiers with beautiful lace for use on the costume of the period.

After the French Revolution, and the death of the King and demise of the aristocracy, any industry was ended. Owing to its scarcity, lace became very valuable and expensive, e.g. in 1867 two flounces of Alençon lace made at Monsieur LeFebure's School cost £3,400.

In England, many poor women gave up domestic service to make lace in their own homes. Although they were poorly paid, fortunes were made by the agents who collected it from the workers, and sold it for large sums. Bedford, Buckingham and Honiton laces were much sought after by ladies of fashion, and even by the Queens of England. King Charles II is reputed to have ordered 600 yards of Buckingham lace to trim his night shirts!

After Thomas Heathcoate invented a machine to make lace and net in 1808, hand-made lace was replaced by machine-made lace—but it was not as beautiful nor as durable as that made by hand.

Although we live in a machine age, many people admire beautiful hand-made articles, and continue to make or buy original craftwork.

The number of lacemakers in England is increasing due to the enthusiasm of Womens' Institutes, Townswomens' Guilds, County Guilds of Craftsmen, etc. Unfortunately, it is very difficult to obtain patterns, or a book of simple instructions.

This book is an attempt to remedy the difficulty, and by progressing in simple and easy stages, the student will gain in knowledge and ability and make many very attractive patterns of traditional lace—and will feel that time has been well spent in creating work of such long lasting beauty.

Amy Dawson
*Bournemouth, 1977*

# Requirements for Lacemaking

You will need the following basic items:

A Pillow

Bobbins to take thread of various thicknesses

Pricking for pattern

Pins—fine and thick brass

Pin cushion

A Pricker and card for the design

## HOW TO MAKE THREE KINDS OF PILLOWS

### 1  Flat (Fig 1(a))

(a)  A piece of plywood or hardboard 18 × 18 in.

(b)  A bag $18\frac{1}{2}$ × $18\frac{1}{2}$ in of strong cotton or unbleached calico. Leave one end open. Push the hardboard into the bag. Fill with chopped hay or straw—pack very tightly, sew up open end and knead until the pad is firm, and even.

(c)  Make a green or turquoise coloured cover bag, and 2 working cloths about 12 × 12 in.

(d)  A piece of green felt 6 × 18 in to place under the pricking.

### 2  Bolster (Fig. 1(b))

(a)  A piece of strong cotton cloth 27 in. square. Join into a tube, and gather one end, using strong thread.

(b)  Cut a circle of plywood, or thick cardboard of 8 in. diameter, and push well down the tube to the gathered-up end.

(c)  Fill the tube with chopped hay or straw (not sawdust as this is too heavy), pack very tightly, keeping the sides free from lumps. Place a second circle of card on top, gather up the end, and fasten off firmly. Sew a circle of material over each end to make a neat finish.

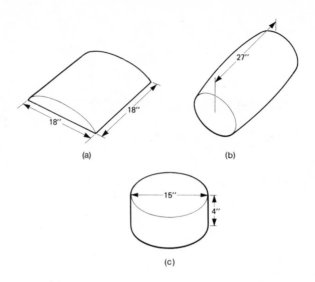

*Fig. 1  Pillows for lacemaking (a) Flat, square (b) Bolster (c) Round
or Honiton*

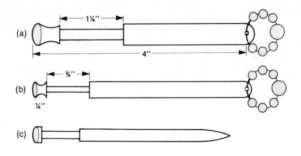

*Fig. 2  Bobbins (a) ³⁄₈ in dowelling for thick thread (b) 5/16 in dowel-
ling for fine thread (c) ¹⁄₄ in dowelling for Honiton thread*

(d) Make a green or turquoise coloured cover 6 in. longer than the bolster, with draw strings through hems of open ends. Make 2 working cloths about 12 × 12 in. of the same material.

(e) Piece of green felt 6 × 26 in. to place under the pricking.

(f) In order to prevent the bolster pillow from rolling about, it is necessary to rest it upon a stand of some kind. The simplest stand can be made from an oblong box, slightly shorter than the pillow, and 3 in. deep. Hollow the sides of the box, so that the pillow will rest firmly in it.

## 3 Round, Honiton (Fig. 1(c))

(a) Two pieces of strong cotton cloth cut into 2 circles of 15 in. diameter.
Four strips 4 × 48 in.—joined into a ring.
Sew together carefully round the edges of circles, leaving a gap for filling.

(b) Fill the cushion with chopped hay or straw, pack until very tight and firm, and close the opening carefully and firmly.

(c) Make a bag slightly larger in green or turquoise cotton. Place over the pillow and sew the ends carefully and neatly.

(d) Make the working cloths 12 × 12 in. of the same material.

(e) A piece of green felt 6 × 14 in. to place under the pricking.

This type of pillow is usually placed on the worker's knees, and the feet on a foot stool for comfort.


## HOW TO MAKE BOBBINS

Three kinds of bobbins are required, and as old bobbins are very expensive and not very easily found in antique shops, it is advisable to make them (Fig. 2).

## 1 Thick thread

Wooden dowelling size $\frac{3}{8}$ in. is best. Cut pieces 4 in. long. With a sharp penknife measure $\frac{3}{8}$ in. for head, and $1\frac{1}{4}$ in. for spool part, which takes the thread. Near to the end bore a small hole. Into this, thread a piece of fine wire with any small beads threaded on to it, usually 7 or 9 according to size. Finish wire ring by joining ends neatly in loops linked together. (see diagram). These beads are called spangles, and act as weights to keep the threads from becoming tangled during work.

Grades 0 and 00 glass paper make the bobbins smooth, but do not varnish, as handling the bobbins gives them an attractive polish. A beginner needs 36, at least.

### 2 Finer thread

Make the bobbins as for the thicker kind—using $^5/_{16}$ in. dowelling. Mark off $^1/_4$ in. for head, and $^3/_4$ in. for spool. Spangles are added made of smallish beads. It is necessary to have 36 fine bobbins at least to start lace edgings.

### 3 Honiton Lace Bobbins

These are made from $^1/_4$ in. dowelling 4 in. long. Mark off $^3/_8$ in. for head and $^3/_4$ in. for spool. With a sharp penknife cut out middle piece until a fine stem is made. Sharpen bottom end on a pencil sharpener. Rub with the finest glass paper until the bobbin is smooth. These have no spangles; 36 bobbins are needed.

### BOBBIN CASES

A bobbin case is a very useful thing to have. A piece of material 18 in. square will hold 36 bobbins. Fold over, (as diagram) and machine at 1 in. intervals, making pockets to hold bobbins, thus preventing threads from tangling and ready for use after being wound with thread (Fig. 3).

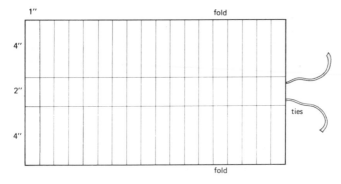

*Fig. 3  A bobbin case for holding 36 bobbins.*

## THREADS

The very best thread for lacemaking is linen in varying thicknesses, but as this is not very easily obtained, crochet cotton makes an excellent substitute, and wears and washes well.

For Honiton lace, fine Sea Island cotton, known as *skip* is used—and a *gimp,* or thicker edging thread, e.g. No. 40 sewing cotton.

## PINS

Very fine and medium thick brass rustless pins are a must. Quite a lot of these are needed, and may be bought in 1-oz tins.

## PIN CUSHIONS

These are made with a loop at one end, to pin on to the pillow in a convenient position. Pins should never be put into the sides of the pillow. This is a bad habit and should be discouraged.

## PATTERNS or PRICKINGS

These are very difficult to find as many designs are destroyed after the lacemaker has died. In this book, I have made drawings of many kinds of lace—thick and fine, and Honiton, the finest of all. If the student works through, from the simplest design to the more complicated, I have graded the work progressively in order of difficulty.

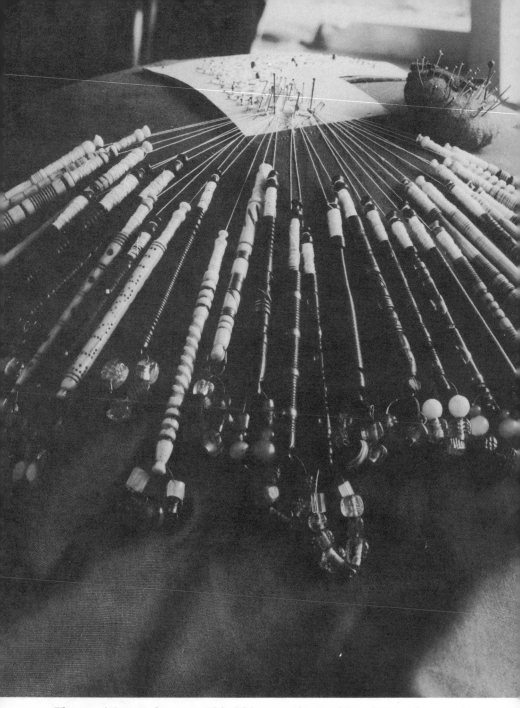

*The position and array of bobbins on the cushion during lacemaking.*
*Note the traditional small strawberry pin-cushion in the top right*
*of the picture.*

# Making Lace

The best way to start learning, is to know how to work the three basic stitches—*whole stitch, half stitch* and *plait*.

The pattern is pricked on to parchment or thick mounting card. First trace Pattern 1 on to tracing paper. Place on a piece of card and prick small holes where indicated. Use a needle, or a proper pricker, made by fixing a needle in a pen holder or piece of dowelling. It is difficult to work patterns with only holes as guides, but it is easier to follow when the lines are drawn in too.

For a long length of lace, the pattern is repeated on to a long strip of card and pinned round the bolster-type pillow. During working, the pillow is turned round in the box or stand, and this does not need to be taken from the pricking, as is the case in shorter designs.

The square pillow is used for corners and larger prickings, as it is easier to manipulate the bobbins on a flatter surface. After the lace has been made, it has to be lifted carefully from the pillow, with the bobbins carefully pinned in the working cloth, in order to repeat the pattern a sufficient number of times.

Place your pricking on to the felt on the flat pillow, and fasten down with long pins at each corner.

### Winding Thread on Bobbins in Pairs

It is not strictly necessary to have a winder, as most lacemakers find it almost as quick to wind bobbins by hand. Bobbins are wound in pairs. Take one bobbin in the left hand with the spool to the right hand side. Lay the end of the thread along the spool for $\frac{1}{2}$ in. and wind on the spool away from your body—moving up and down, smoothly and evenly. Do not fill the bobbin so full that thread projects beyond the edges at the top and bottom. Secure the thread with a *half-hitch* to prevent the thread unwinding. Place the thread round the left thumb and slip it over the head of the bobbin twice, to make a half-hitch. Now pull several yards of thread from ball and then cut off. Wind the second bobbin and make a half-hitch to secure it. Winding bobbins in pairs this way renders knots unnecessary and is a particularly useful method to use where two ends of a piece of lace have to be joined, as it halves the number of ends to be fastened off.

## THE THREE FOUNDATION STITCHES

To learn the three basic stitches, we will work on the sampler, Pattern 1.
First take a tracing of Pattern 1 and prick on to fine card. Draw in the guide lines. Pin the pricking to the pillow at each corner to secure it. Wind 16 bobbins, in pairs, with No. 20 crochet cotton. Place a pin in each of dots indicated. Now hang 1 pair of bobbins on 5 dots (A, B, C, D, E) and another pair at side (called 2 workers).

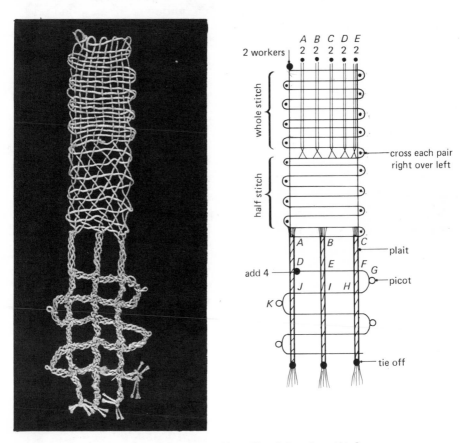

*Pattern 1 A sampler incorporating the 3 basic stitches.*

16

The 10 bobbins hanging straight down are called *passives* and the *workers* work across and back again using each pair of passives in turn.

Work 9 rows whole stitch as indicated in pattern.

**Whole Stitch** or cloth stitch (Fig. 4)

Name the workers 1 and 2, and the first two passives 3 and 4. Pick up 2 and place over 3, take 2 over 1, 4 over 3, and 2 over 3. This is a complete *pass*.

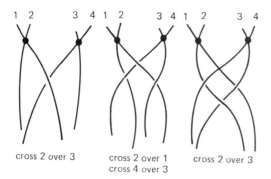

Fig. 4 *The Whole Stitch, one pass*

Continue in this way taking the 2 workers over the next 2 passives until you have worked once across pattern.
*Twist* workers once, i.e. right over left, put *a pin up*, slanting slightly outwards.
Wrap the workers round the pin, twist once more and continue working whole stitch from right to left.
Repeat the twist round another pin and repeat for nine rows. This stitch looks like open darning—hence sometimes called cloth stitch. The next 9 rows are worked in *half stitch*, the second of the basic stitches.

**Half Stitch** (Fig. 5)

First cross each pair of passives from right to left.

Fig. 5 *The Half Stitch.*

cross right over left to begin

Now with the workers, take No. 2 over 3, 2 over 1, 4 over 3, and pass on to next pair of passives.
Continue to right edge—twist, put a pin up, twist, and return across to left edge. This stitch is exactly like whole stitch except that 3 moves are made by the workers instead of 4. This looks like lattice work instead of plain weaving.

Continue to make half stitch until indicated by the pattern pricking.

Now draw 2 passives and 2 workers together and put a pin at A ready for the *plait stitch*.
Draw the centre 4 bobbins and place a pin at B, and again with the remaining 4 at C.

### Plait Stitch (Fig. 6)

With the 4 bobbins at A make a plait thus. Make *3 complete passes* with only the 4 bobbins, put a pin between the 4 bobbins and leave.
Continue to make 3 or more plaits at B and C.
Now at point D, hang on 2 more pairs of bobbins. These will make *plaited workers* and travel across B and C plaits as indicated in pattern.

Make a whole stitch with 4 pairs bobbins at D, work 3 plaits across to E.
*Cross plaits* by making half stitch, put pin up, and close, by 2 over 3.
Continue in the same way to F, with 4 working plaits, work 4 plait stitches, place a pin at G, take the extreme left bobbin, loop thread over pin for *Picot*.

*Fig. 6 The Plait Stitch with picots.*

Continue plaiting across, working through the three passive plaits.

Finish the sampler (Pattern 1) by plaiting 4 times on 3 passive plaits. Cut off threads and tie 3 times carefully.
You can now proceed with the first lace edging, all plaits and picots. This is Le Puy Plaited Lace, Pattern 2.

## LE PUY PLAITED LACE

Make a pricking of Pattern 2, plaited lace. Wind 14 large bobbins with No. 20 Crochet Cotton. Place a pin at A and hang on 4 bobbins. Make 3 plait stitches to (a), place a pin and make a picot, 3 plait stitches and leave on a pin at (b) to wait.

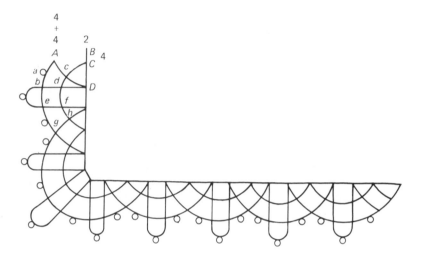

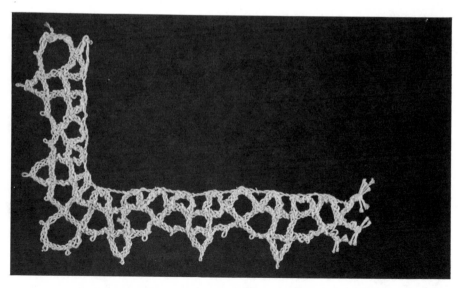

*Pattern 2  Le Puy plaited lace*

Place 4 more bobbins on A and work 4 plaits to (c), leave on a pin.
Put 2 bobbins on a pin at B. Twist twice and leave to hang down for
the edge.
Place 4 bobbins on a pin at C, work 3 plaits, and cross plait with 4
bobbins waiting at (c).
Make 3 plaits with left hand 4 bobbins, put a pin in at (d) and leave.
With right hand 4 bobbins plait 3 times, make a whole stitch with 2
edge bobbins, D, put a pin up, make another whole stitch, and work 3
plaits and cross plait with bobbins waiting at (d).
Continue plaiting with working bobbins, and cross plait at (b).
Work 3 plaits and put a pin up at (e) to wait.
With working bobbins now work 4 plaits, make a picot, and work 4
more plaits and cross plait at (e).
Work 3 plaits and cross plait at (f). Work 4 plaits, connect at edge
with 2 bobbins, put up a pin, work the whole stitch once more.

From (e), work 3 plait, make a picot and 3 plaits pin in at (g) and
leave.
From (f) work 3 plaits, put a pin at (h).

With the 4 bobbins left at edge, plait 4, cross plait at (h) plait 3 and
cross plait at (g).

This is one completed pattern.

Repeat—following corner design and work as many patterns as required before making another corner.

All the plaits should be tight and firm to make a good piece of lace.


## LACE PATTERN 3

Make a pricking from Pattern 3—the practise pattern for a Cluny
edge. Wind 20 bobbins in pairs and No. 20 crochet cotton.

Start at left edge, hanging a pair of bobbins on each of 4 indicated
positions.
Take the working pair, make a whole stitch with first passive pair,
twist once, whole stitch with 2nd and 3rd pairs with one twist be-
tween.
Place a pin at A, make another whole stitch, and work through 2nd
and 3rd pairs of passives.
Turn at B and across in the same way to C. Put a pin up to wait.
Hang 4 bobbins at D—plait 3 and put a pin up at E.
Hang another 4 bobbins at E, plait 3, and join to 2 workers at C.
This is done by working a whole stitch with 2 workers and the four
bobbins of the plait.

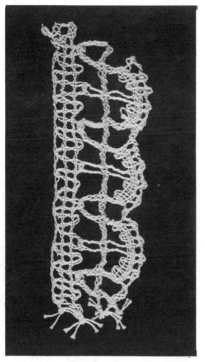

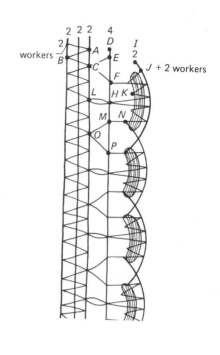

*Pattern 3 Practise for Cluny edge*

Put up a pin—make another whole stitch.
Continue working the left edge with 2 workers, going backwards and forwards through the passives, and joining to right hand plaits.
Make 3 plaits from E to F, and 3 plaits from C to F.
Cross plait, work 3 plaits from F to G, put a pin up and wait.
Plait 3 and leave on a pin at H.

At the right hand scallop edge, pin 2 bobbins for edge passives, at I, and 2 workers at J.
Work a whole stitch with J workers through I edge pair.
Twist workers once. Take a pin out at G—work a whole stitch with opened out plait threads—2 at a time.
Replace pin at G, work whole stitch back across 4 threads.
Twist once, make a whole stitch through edge pair, put a pin up, work a whole stitch.
Twist once—work across scallop to K, put pin at K, work whole stitch back to edge and return in the same way to centre.
Twist workers 3 times, work whole stitch at H, twist twice, and join to inner edge workers with a whole stitch at L.

21

*Le Puy braid lace edging on a table mat.*

Twist twice and work another whole stitch at H.
Twist 3 times and continue to work whole stitch through scallop to edge, back again to centre, out again to the edge, back again to N.
Work whole stitch, put in a pin, the workers return to the outer edge, but the whole stitch scallop threads form a 3 plait to M.
Cross plait at M, with plait of 3 from H.
Work a 4 plait, and put a pin at P with the other 4 bobbins make a plait of 3 from M to O and from O to P.

This completes a whole pattern. Continue in the same way round corner and for as many scallops as required between the corners. The four threads of a plait are often opened out in this way to form scallops, in many designs. The 3 pairs of passive bobbins make an attractive and firm straight edge called the 'head' of the lace.

## MAJORCA PLAITED LACE

Make a pricking from Pattern 3a.

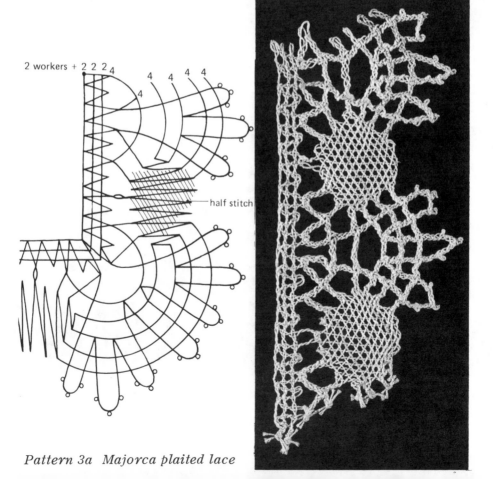

*Pattern 3a   Majorca plaited lace*

*An attractive use of Majorca lace incorporating an original corner design by the author.*

Wind 32 bobbins with No. 20 cotton.

Hang bobbins where shown, and start at left side with 2 workers making whole stitches through each of 3 pairs of passives, and with a twist between each.

The plaits are made as in earlier patterns, until the half stitch circle is reached, when the left pair of bobbins to begin this is turned into a pair of workers, travelling across and back in half-stitch.

After you have made lace Pattern 2 at the beginning, the plait will not be difficult to work.

This is an easy and very attractive lace to make. It is very useful for table mats, tray cloths, etc.

It is interesting to note that, in the past, a lacemaker traditionally only learned one pattern of lace, and it was passed from mother to daughter, from generation after generation. I was able to get this design from a very old lady in the Spanish Village in Palma, Majorca. She only made the straight yards of lace for sale, but I made a corner pattern for it.

# Lace Grounds, Spiders, Blocks and Leaves

## LACE GROUNDS

### Torchon, or Reseau Ground

Make pricking from Pattern 4.

Wind 20 bobbins with No. 20 crochet cotton.

Hang 4 bobbins on pins at (a), (b), (c), (d), and (e).

Twist 2nd and 3rd pair once, make a half stitch, put pin at 1 and cross No. 2 over 3 to close the stitch.

Twist 1st and 2nd pair once, make a half stitch, put a pin at 2, twist each pair once and leave.

Take the other pair at (b) and one pair at (c) twist each pair once, make a half stitch, put a pin at 3, and close stitch.

Twist each pair once and leave.

These crossed pairs of bobbins make the torchon stitch.

Now take a pair from 1 and a pair from 3 and make torchon stitch at 4.

Take one pair from 2 and a pair from 4 and make torchon stitch at 5.

Take a pair from 2 and a pair from 5 make edge stitch at 6 and leave.

With a pair from (c) and a pair from (d), make torchon stitch at 7, and continue to work diagonally to 8, 9, 10, 11, and 12.

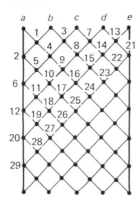

*Pattern 4  Basic Torchon ground*

With a pair from (d) and (e), work from 13 to 20.
Keep left and right edges straight by pulling threads down gently each time they are reached.
Work several rows in this way until you are familiar with the stitch. In making Torchon Lace you will be working more in diagonal lines than horizontal ones.

## Dieppe

Make a pricking from Pattern 4 as for Torchon.
This stitch is worked in exactly the same way as Torchon stitch but with two twists between pins instead of a single twist. In this way a stronger ground is made.

## Net

Use the same pricking as for previous 2 patterns and wind 20 bobbins as before. This is also worked diagonally, but bobbins are twisted 3 times, between crossings. A *Crossing* is passing the inside bobbin of the left pair over the inside bobbin of the right pair, the outside bobbins remaining passive. The movement requires both hands and both pairs of bobbins.
When a crossing has been made a pin is put in under the threads but not between them.

## Brussels

Use the same pricking as for previous patterns.
20 bobbins are required and hung on pins at (a), (b), (c), (d), and (e), as before.
The bobbins are twisted twice, and where they meet, two plaits are worked, even at the side edges. The pins are placed between the plaits.
This ground is also worked diagonally.

## Rose

Make a pricking of Pattern 5.
Wind 24 bobbins with No. 20 cotton.
Hang two bobbins at A and two at B. Twist twice, make a half stitch and one extra twist.
Repeat with 2 bobbins at C and D.
With the two middle pairs make a half stitch and an extra twist.
Put a pin at 1.
Enclose pin with a half stitch and an extra twist.

27

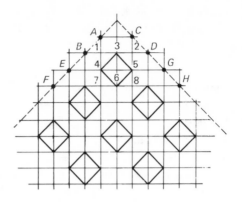

*Pattern 5  Rose ground*

With the two left-hand pairs, make a half stitch and an extra twist.
Put a pin in 2 and enclose the pin with a half stitch and an extra
twist.
With the two right-hand bobbins make a half stitch and an extra
twist.
Put a pin in 3.
Enclose pin with a half stitch and an extra twist.
With the two middle pairs, make a half stitch and an extra twist.
Put a pin in 4.
Enclose pin with a half stitch and an extra twist. A half stitch and an
extra twist are used between each group of holes.
As this filling is worked diagonally, the next bobbins are added at
E and F with the right-hand two pairs coming from 2 and 4.
After the second square has been worked on the left-hand, two bob-
bins are added at G and H, to work square on the right-hand side.
It will be seen that the squares are made with a space between each.

### SPIDERS, BLOCKS AND LEAVES

**Dieppe** (with little spiders)

Make a pricking of Pattern 6.
Wind 20 bobbins with No. 20 cotton.
Hang 4 bobbins at a, b, c, d, and e.
Work Dieppe stitch until 19. Twist the pairs from 14, 15, 18 and 19,
three times.
The two pairs on the left side pass through those on the right in
whole stitch.
A pin is put up in the centre hole, the four pairs are pulled into

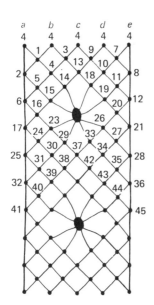

*Pattern 6  Dieppe ground,
with spiders*

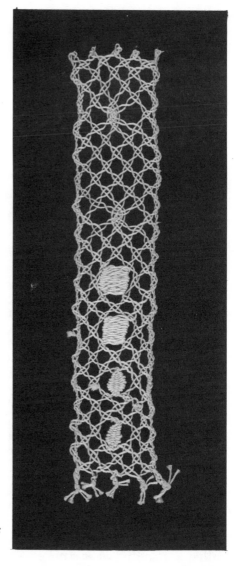

*Sample ground
with spiders, blocks
and leaves*

position and then the threads are all crossed again in whole stitch, twisting each three times before being taken into the groundwork. Continue until 45 and make the second spider as before.

On many Torchon patterns, larger spiders are made (with more legs) in the same way as the four-legged ones just made.

29

**Torchon** (with Block Stitch)

Make a pricking of Pattern 7.
Wind 24 bobbins with No. 20 cotton.

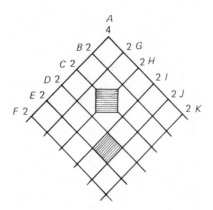

*Pattern 7 Torchon with blocks*

Hang four bobbins at A and two on each of B, C, D, E, F, G, H, I, J, and K.

Work Torchon stitch for ground until block is made.

Take two pairs of bobbins in the left hand, spread three threads wide apart. Using the thread on extreme right as a worker, weave under the middle thread, back under the first, over the second, under the 3rd, and weaving backwards and forwards, not too tightly or the square will be spoiled.

Having worked the desired amount of passes, twist the pairs once and continue the background, until next block is required.

In some patterns, the block is worked sideways, so instead of the pairs on left and right being used to weave on, two pairs on the left are used and the weaving stitch worked in the same way as the upright block.

This filling is also used in Cluny and Honiton Lace, and is often called spot stitch when worked in very fine cotton.

**Torchon** (with leaves)

Make a pricking of Pattern 8.
Wind 16 bobbins with No. 20 cotton.
Work Torchon stitch until A, make a whole stitch and put a pin at A.
Take three of the bobbins in the left hand, spread open, and with the fourth bobbin on the right, weave under the middle thread, back

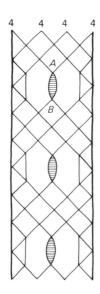

*Pattern 8  Torchon with leaves*

under the first, over the second, and under the third. Keep the three threads taut in the left hand, allowing the weaving bobbin to regulate the shape of the leaf. At the end of the leaf, make a whole stitch and put up a pin at B.

Continue with torchon background until another leaf is made.

These leaves are used a great deal in Cluny, Bedford and other laces.

When two or more leaves are joined in a design, a whole stitch is made, but if the threads need to be crossed, a half stitch is made, with two threads acting as one thread, a pin is put up and closed.

Often the groups of four threads continue to make another leaf.

# The Family of Lace

## TORCHON LACE

This lace is of Continental origin and was very popular in the past because of its many uses.

The patterns are many and various, from the heavy type to the fine and delicate.

An ancient name for it was *Gueuse,* meaning beggar-woman's lace. The main characteristics are its background and varieties of scallop, on the outer edge.

The addition of leaves, blocks, spiders, zig-zags, squares and diamonds in whole and half stitch, give numerous very fine patterns, many of which came from Malta, Saxony, parts of France and Spain.

Most lacemakers enjoy making Torchon Lace, as it gives excellent results quickly, and it can be used for numerous personal and household articles.


### Plain Pattern Torchon Lace

Wind 18 bobbins with No. 20 cotton.
Make a pricking of Pattern 9.
Hang 4 bobbins at A, B and C, and two bobbins and two workers at D.

Start at the right-hand side with two workers, make a whole stitch with the 2 passives from D. Make a twist, work 2 whole stitches with the four from C. Make a twist and with the right-hand pair from B, work a Torchon stitch at F. Make a twist, work two whole stitches through 4 passives and make a twist. Make a whole stitch through 2 passives, put in a pin at G, and return through the two and the four edge passives to wait at H.
Now with two bobbins from A and two from B, make a Torchon stitch at E. With two bobbins from F, and two from E, make a torchon stitch at I, and with two from I and two from G, make a torchon stitch at H. Make a twist and work across four and two passives to K.
Work back from K to R, and leave on a pin.

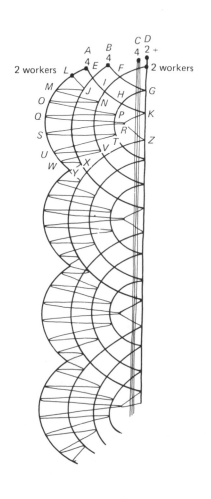

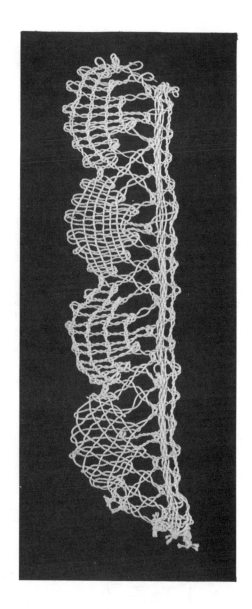

*Pattern 9  Plain Torchon lace*

Now with two bobbins from A and two workers from L, make a whole stitch. Make two twists and a whole stitch with two bobbins from E. Put a pin at J. This begins *the Shell edge*.

With two twists between each whole stitch, the workers travel to and fro from right to left taking in pairs at N, P and R, and sending out pairs at R, T, V, X and Y.

It will soon be seen that this pattern is worked in two parts, a scallop and *a triangle of Torchon stitches*. The corner is a continuation of the pattern, but with two scallops instead of one.

This design may be varied by having only a single twist between the scallop passives, or with whole or half stitch scallops.

### Torchon with Half Stitch Scallop

Wind 20 bobbins with No. 20 cotton.

Make a pricking of Pattern 10.

Hang two pairs of passives and one pair of workers below A. Hang three pairs at B and two pairs at C and D. Begin at the left edge by making a whole stitch with the first pair. Make a twist and a whole stitch with the second pair. Now cross each of other pairs right over left ready for the half stitch.

Work a half stitch across to D. Make two twists, put pin up, and work back to I, leaving one pair to go to 9 through the two passives of the foot of lace. Continue to work a half stitch for the scallop, leaving one pair out at 3, 5 and 7 to make the Torchon triangle.

After working to 8, continue with the half stitch scallop, taking in pairs from the left to 18, as this completes the pattern.

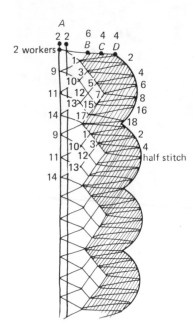

*Pattern 10   Torchon with half
              stitch scallop*

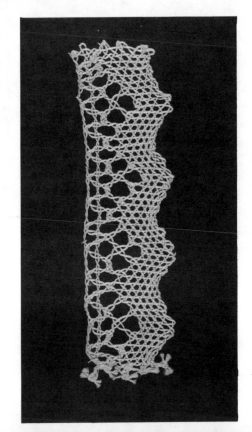

## Torchon with Spider and Shell

Make a pricking from Pattern 11.
Wind 30 bobbins with No. 20 cotton.
Hang four bobbins at B and at G and two bobbins at A, C, D, E, F, H, I, J, K, L and M.
Start working at D, make torchon stitch with a pair at C, make a whole stitch through 4 passives, twist once, make a whole stitch with the edge pair. Put a pin up and make another whole stitch. Now take in new pairs and work torchon stitch, until the Spider is reached in centre of pattern, moving to the right where a scallop is made in a whole stitch.

The corner spider has two legs at one side, and three at the other, but the pattern continues as for the straight lace.

*Pattern 11  Torchon with spiders and shell*

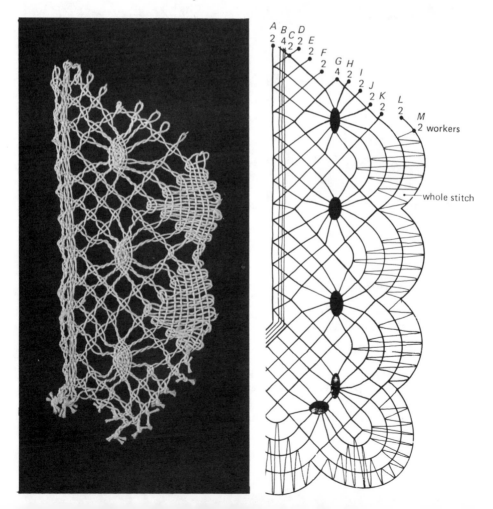

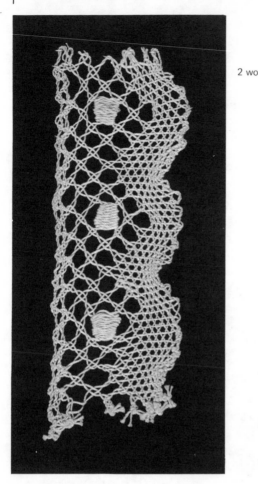
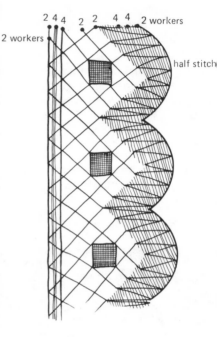

*Pattern 12   Torchon with blocks*

### Torchon with Block

Make a pricking from Pattern 12.

Wind 26 bobbins with No. 20 cotton.

Hang bobbins where indicated, starting at the straight edge on the left.

There are two and four passive pairs with a twist between them for the foot of this pattern, torchon stitch for the centre part, and half stitch scallop.

The block is worked as in the background Pattern 7.

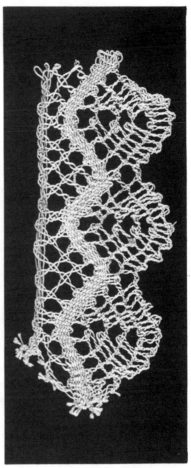

*Pattern 13   Torchon with zig-zag*

## Torchon with Zig-Zag in Whole Stitch (or half stitch)

Make a pricking from Pattern 13.
Wind 30 bobbins with No. 20 cotton.
Hang bobbins where indicated, starting at the straight edge on the left.
There are four passives close together, worked in whole stitch for the foot of this pattern. At D, hang on two workers and eight passives, to form plain band.
After working a whole stitch across, add two bobbins for passives in the shell at E.

37

Work across and back, when two more bobbins are added. The next two pairs of shell passives come from the torchon stitch. It will be seen in this pattern that pairs of bobbins are taken into the zig-zag band on the left, and pairs are passed out into the shell pattern, and vice-versa.

The corner should present no difficulty. Proceed as for the edging.

**Torchon Insertion**

With rose background, zig-zags in whole stitch, half stitch, Spiders, and whole stitch scallops.

Make a pricking from Pattern 14(a).

Wind 48 bobbins with No. 40 cotton.

Hang bobbins where shown on pattern, starting at the left side, and as all the stitches have been learned already, this design presents a challenge.

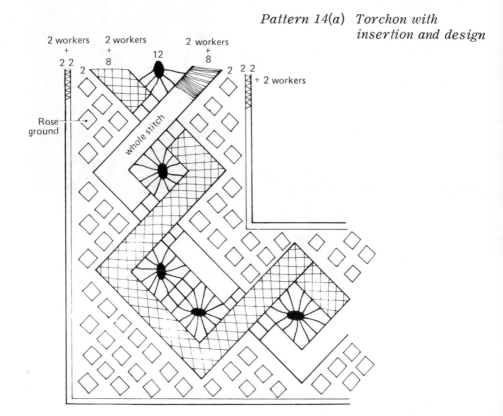

*Pattern 14(a)   Torchon with insertion and design*

All complicated patterns are a combination of various stitches used in previous laces. If the portions of the design are built up slowly, the student will enjoy puzzling out even the widest patterns.

**Lace Edging to Match Insertion**

Make a pricking from Pattern 14(b).
Wind 48 bobbins with No. 40 cotton.
Hang bobbins where indicated, and work out the design piece by piece like the insertion. Use these two pieces of lace together to make a lovely table cloth.

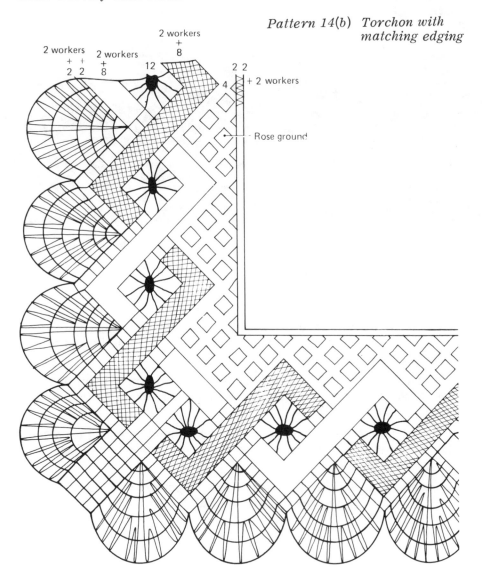

*Pattern 14(b) Torchon with matching edging*

*An example of Cluny lace with a scalloped inner edge.*

### CLUNY LACE

The designs for this lace are a little more elaborate than Torchon and usually for thick thread, but may be worked in fine thread to great advantage.

It is understood that many laces received their names from the places where they were made, e.g. Maltese lace from Malta, Bedford lace from Bedford, etc.

Several types of stitches combine to make Cluny lace, and its name may have referred originally to copies of old lace in the Musée Cluny in Paris.

There are no new stitches to learn, but the patterns are arranged in such a way that the results are very attractive.

The prickings given here, will enable the pupil to make a wide variety of lace and enjoy the results.

The five main patterns are described below.

### Edging Pattern

With half stitch band and leaves.
Make a pricking from Pattern 15.
Wind 30 bobbins with No. 20 cotton.

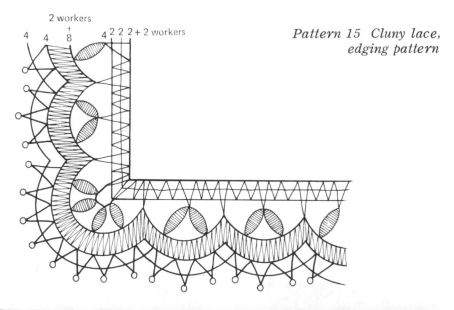

*Pattern 15   Cluny lace,*
*edging pattern*

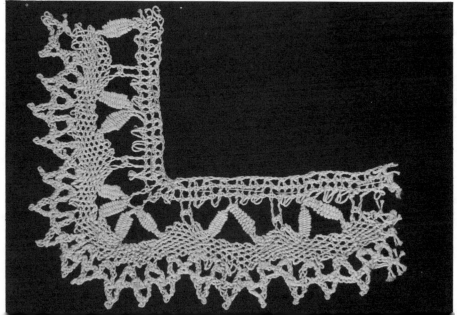

Hang bobbins where indicated, starting at the straight edge at the right.

There are three passives with a twist between, for the foot of this pattern, starting with two workers on the right. After working through the three passives, four bobbins are joined on for the leaf, and left on a pin, to be taken into band later.

For the band, two workers make half stitch across eight passives, take in four more for plait, which forms the scallop edge on the left.

The workers from the foot, and the workers from the band connect the parts of the pattern when they meet.

As the thread is thick, 3 twists are needed to make picots.

**Wider Edging**

With whole stitch band, flowers and half stitch medallions.

Make a pricking from Pattern 16.

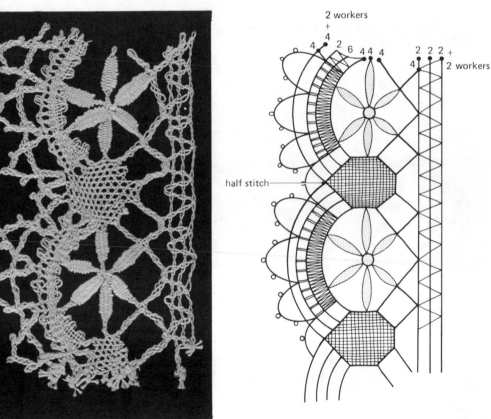

*Pattern 16  Cluny wider edging pattern*

Wind 40 bobbins with No. 20 cotton.

Hang bobbins where indicated, starting at the left with the whole stitch band.

The workers make a whole stitch with the first two passives, twist once and work in whole stitch through eight passives. Take in four bobbins on right, work across and take in another four on the left for plait.

The picots are twisted three times and the leaves, making flowers, are joined in the centre by whole stitches. It will be noticed that the band has an edge of two bobbins with a twist between. Thus, we are making an attractive variation from the usual plain band.

To make the half stitch medallion, use the left-hand pair of bobbins from the leaf, to act as workers, taking in four bobbins from the right hand side and then four bobbins from the left until the centre is reached, when four bobbins are cast away to form plaits, or to pass into the band or to make a leaf.

**Wide Edging Pattern**

With four extra bobbins added and removed at a later stage.
Make a pricking from Pattern 17.
Wind 48 bobbins with No. 20 cotton (4 extra bobbins are needed).
Hang bobbins where indicated, four at A (two passives and two workers), two at B, two at C, four at (c), twelve at D (four for leaf and four at each side for plaits), four at E, six at F, and two workers, four at each of G, H, I.

Begin at A, with two workers, making whole stitches through the three passives, with a twist between. Join in four bobbins at c for plait, which then makes a leaf. At D, make a whole stitch with twelve bobbins, the left four make a plait to picot on the left-side of centre leaf, and right-hand four plait to picot on the right.
Make a plait with double picot from E. With two workers at F, make a whole stitch through six passives for braid, twist twice and connect with four threads at G, twist twice and work through braid again. The four bobbins at I make a plait which works through plaits from H and G, and is joined to the two workers from the braid. The plait from G works through H plait, and forms loop with picots, which continues along edge of lace scallop.

Now make centre flower, by making a leaf from D, put a pin in centre and leave until leaves from left and right are made.
For centre of flower, use the left-hand pair of bobbins from pin in 1st leaf as workers, make whole stitch through second pair, take in four bobbins from right-hand leaf, put pin up and work back in

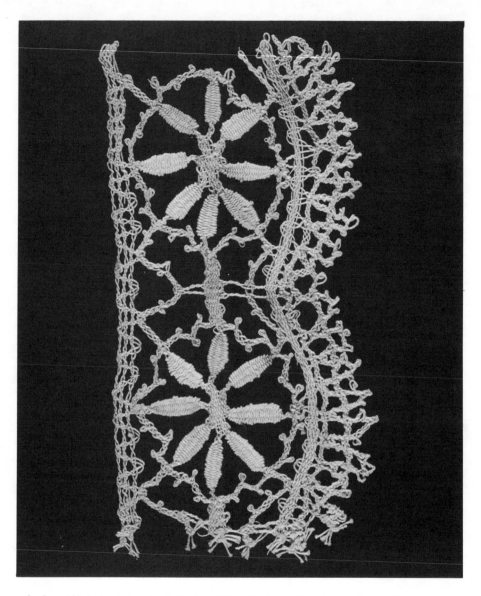

whole stitch to take in left-hand leaf. In order to make a firm whole stitch centre in the flower, it is best to work across and back once more before adding four bobbins to make new leaf on left side of pattern.

The plait with picots, and the two workers from the foot of lace meet at point where four new bobbins are added. The workers go

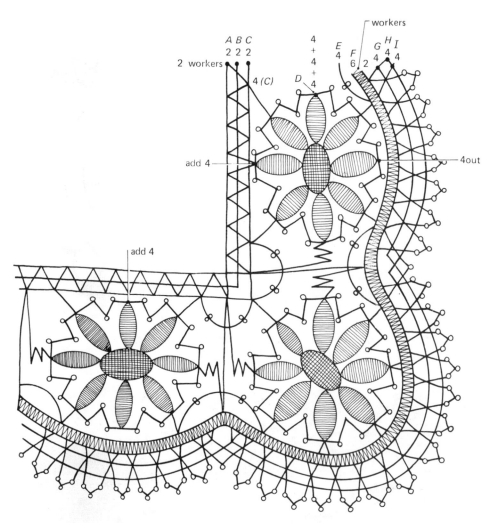

*Pattern 17  Cluny wide edging pattern*

through the plait 1st and then take in the extra four for leaf. The workers go into flower centre and then move out to make right-hand leaf, join to plait and tie off to be cut off and darned in later. Work whole stitch across flower centre and back before making another leaf, using four bobbins from the centre, joining plait and making a plait with double picots, and joining in with workers from foot, then another plait with picots, put in a pin and leave to be taken into runners at end of pattern.

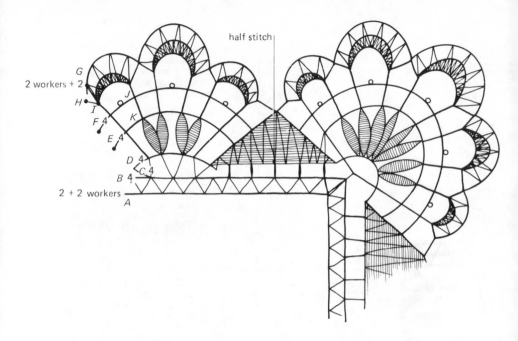

**half stitch**

G
2 workers + 2
H
I
J
F 4
E 4
K
D 4
B 4 C 4
2 + 2 workers
A

*Pattern 18   Cluny half stitch triangle*

Return to flower centre where four more bobbins are taken out to make a right-hand leaf, join plait, make a plait, to be joined in braid and out to form curved plait between designs.

The last four bobbins in the flower make the final leaf, meeting the two plaits, where a band of whole stitch is made with two workers and ten passives.

Half way, the two workers twist 5 times make whole stitch with plait, twist three times, join to edge workers, returning with three twists, through plait again, twist five times, make whole stitch through band, twist three times, whole stitch through plait, twist twice, join braid, twist twice, through plait, twist three times, through band of whole stitch and ending in a plait to form a leaf in the corner design.

The corner is continued in the same pattern, and working to a straight pattern once more.

### Half Stitch Triangle Pattern

Make a pricking of Pattern 18.
Wind 28 bobbins with No. 40 or No. 20 cotton.
Hang four bobbins at A, (two passives and two workers) make a whole stitch put pin in, twist once, work whole stitch through four at B, put pin in, work to take in the plait from C, cross the plait from D, E and F. Make two twists with pair of bobbins from G, whole stitch with pair from H, which are the workers on the scallop. These workers meet the plait at 1, and open out the 4 threads with wh. st, working back and forth to J, where a plait is formed again.

It will be noted that plait from F has a picot half way across to meet plait from J. At K, the plait becomes a leaf, joining with plait which started at D, put pin up. Another leaf is made with the same four bobbins used for 1st leaf, but the four plaited threads divide into twos, twisting three times to join workers in foot of lace, returning to meet centre 2 which are twisted twice and meet again after the third leaf has been made. Make a plait once more.
Continue to work the second part of scallop, until the half stitch triangle.

Take the left-hand pair of bobbins from the middle plait and use these as workers, keeping the right-hand side straight, connecting every other row to foot and taking four bobbins in on the left every alternate row.

Pattern 19  *Cluny inner scallop pattern*

After the apex of triangle has been reached, four bobbins are taken out to make plaits again for start of corner.

The two pairs of workers from the triangle and the foot meet with whole stitch and part, making a bar across every other row.

The corner of this design presents no further difficulty. Extra care must be taken to make the leaves even and the same size throughout the pattern.

## Inner Scallop Pattern

Make a pricking of Pattern 19.
Wind 28 bobbins with No. 20 cotton.
Hang on bobbins where indicated, starting at the right.
The two workers make a whole stitch through the four passives. Make a twist and whole stitch with the end pair. Put up a pin, twist two workers and leave on the right, taking the end pair as workers to travel back into pattern. This will keep a straight edge on the right-hand scallop. This must be done every time the workers meet throughout the pattern.

This design is so much like the previous one that the student will find no difficulty in working it.

When mounting this lace to linen, it is advisable to work Punch stitch.


## FINE LACE

Having worked with thick bobbins and thick thread, it is now time to work in Nos. 80 and 100 cotton and *finer bobbins*.

All the stitches and backgrounds are the same, so the finer patterns should present no difficulty. The stitches are drawn on to the patterns, the number of bobbins required and just where to start the pattern is also marked.

Bedford and Maltese laces are seldom worked in thick thread, and it will be noted that picots are now *pearls* (with five twists of the threads). This creates a very dainty and beautiful lace for handkerchiefs and trimmings generally.

When making a handkerchief, it is much more satisfactory if fine linen is bought by the yard and lace mounted as described in the special chapter on this subject.

To add hand-made lace to a machine made article, such as a tray cloth, table cloth or handkerchief, detracts considerably from its beauty and value.

The eight main patterns of fine lace are given below.

**Fine Le Puy Plait**

Pattern 20 is a finer version of the first one learned.
Wind 14 *thin bobbins* with No. 80 cotton.
Work exactly as for thick design, making plaits even and not too tight.

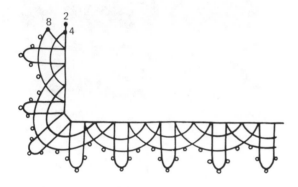

*Pattern 20   Fine Le Puy plaited lace*

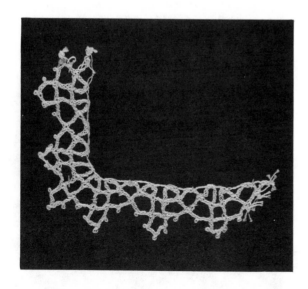

## Le Puy Plaited Lace with Leaves

Pattern 21 is similar to Pattern 20 but with small leaves which must be worked evenly to ensure the final attractive lace.
It is advisable to continue to make a square of this lace and make a handkerchief, as this gives the student a sense of achievement.

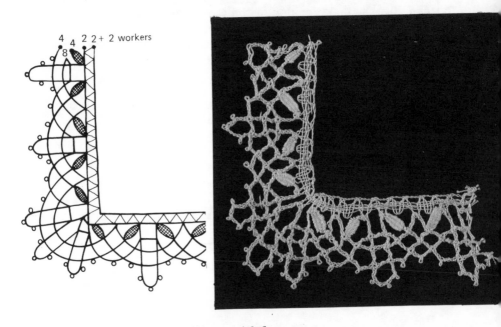

*Pattern 21  Le Puy plaited lace with leaves*

*Pattern 22  Torchon with whole stitch triangle*

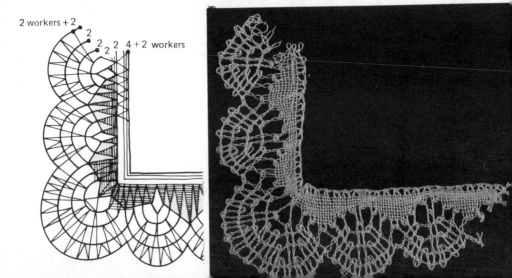

## Torchon with Whole Stitch Triangle

As this (Pattern 22) is like other torchons, it is very attractive in finer thread. Try to keep the whole stitch tight and the passives straight in order to work the plain triangle.

## Cluny with Half Stitch Triangle

There is no need to explain Pattern 23 as it is a fine version of the thick lace made earlier.

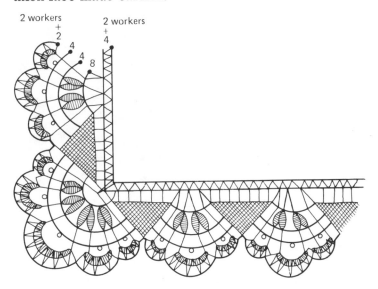

*Pattern 23   Cluny with half stitch triangle*

## Maltese Insertion

The beauty of Pattern 24 relies on leaves and pearls which must be carefully worked or the effect is lost entirely.

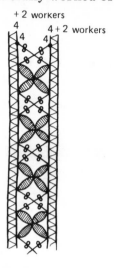

*Pattern 24   The Maltese insertion*

## Maltese Lace to Match Insertion

Pattern 25 will present no difficulty as the edging is similar to the insertion, but with looped edging. Used in conjunction with the insertion, it will make delightful trimming for children's clothing.

*Pattern 25   Maltese lace to match the insertion*

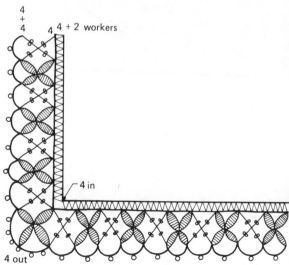

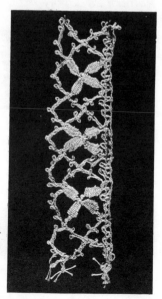

## Bedford Handkerchief

It will be seen that eight bobbins are added to outerbraid on beginning the pattern and again on working the corner.
Four bobbins are hung on a pin as marked on pattern, and a whole stitch with the workers connects them to enter the pattern.

When taking bobbins out of Pattern 26, let them lie to one side until a little more of the pattern has been worked, when they are knotted in pairs and the threads cut off leaving about 3 in. of thread. This must be darned in later to neaten the lace.

*Pattern 26*
  *Bedford handkerchief*

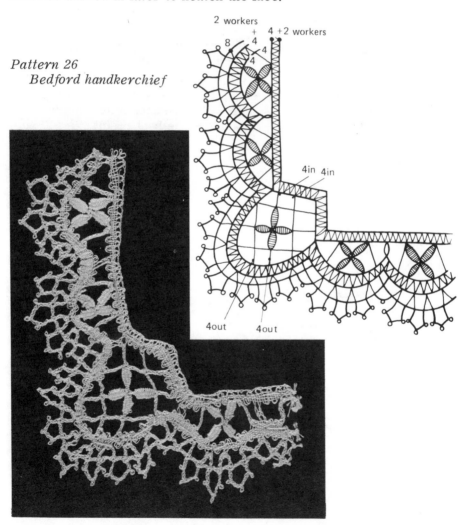

## Bedford 'Fertility' Handkerchief

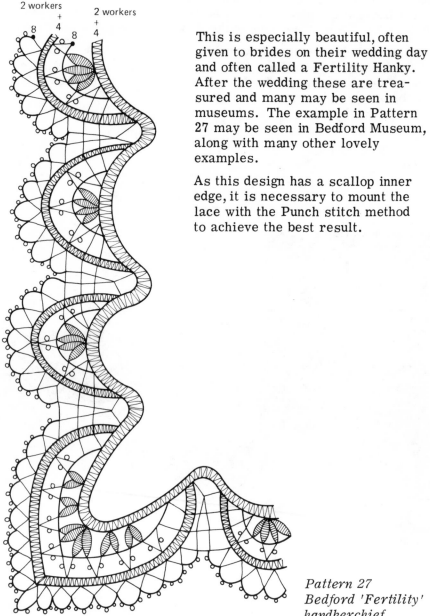

2 workers
+
4

8    4    8

2 workers
+
4

This is especially beautiful, often given to brides on their wedding day and often called a Fertility Hanky. After the wedding these are treasured and many may be seen in museums. The example in Pattern 27 may be seen in Bedford Museum, along with many other lovely examples.

As this design has a scallop inner edge, it is necessary to mount the lace with the Punch stitch method to achieve the best result.

*Pattern 27*
*Bedford 'Fertility'*
*handkerchief*

## Special Note

At this stage, it is necessary to mention that many irregularities in the prickings may be noticed, but as all my patterns are from traditional designs, this often happens.

If, however, the student wishes to have more accurate prickings, these can be worked out on graph paper.

Lace made on these designs can be more accurate, but lose that Hand-made look which is part of its charm.

## RUSSIAN LACE

The so-called Russian lace is not of Russian origin at all, yet despite its late introduction there, Russia has now most claim to this lace; not only are most Russian laces of this kind, but comparatively little is made elsewhere.

This lace is different from other types of pillow-lace which we have been working on. It is entirely composed of one or more narrow braids which form the whole pattern of straight and curved lines connected at short intervals by small loops of thread.

The commonest form of braid used in Russian lace is a simple cloth stitch band, or a double band with two pairs of workers which meet and part again.

Not many bobbins are needed for this lace, thick braid was used for Old Flanders Lace, but fine cotton makes more delicate lace for edgings, collars and mats.

Although this is not a very popular lace, it is advisable to include a few designs in case anyone cares to try it out.

Many students might like to make their own patterns to suit their own requirements.

### Russian Plain Braid

Make a pricking of Pattern 28.
Wind 12 thick bobbins with No. 20 cotton.
Hang six bobbins at A, four at B and two at C.
Start at B, with a whole stitch, put a pin up, make one twist, work a whole stitch through each pair at A. Make one twist, and a whole stitch with the pair at C. Put a pin up and make another whole stitch. Make a twist and work across to 2. Make a whole stitch, put a pin up, and make another whole stitch before working across again.

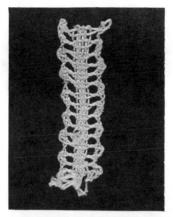

*Pattern 28   Russian plain braid*

This double whole stitch at each side is necessary when two braids meet and are joined by a crochet hook.

### Russian Waved Braid

Make a pricking of Pattern 29.
Wind 14 bobbins with No. 20 cotton.

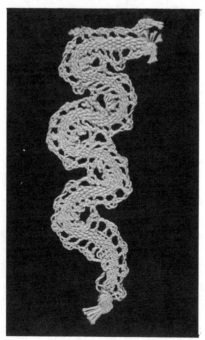

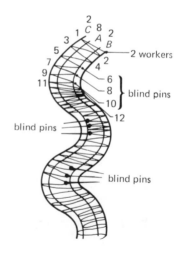

*Pattern 29   Russian waved braid*

Hang eight bobbins at A, four at B and two at C.

Work across with two workers from B, as for plain braid, passing from 1 to 2, 3, 4, 5, to 6, when workers turn back without going through end pair.

Put a pin up where indicated and return to 7, then back to 8. Put a pin up and work to 9, 10 and 11. At 12, take in the edge pair once more. Positions 6, 8, and 10 are known as *blind pins* and help to form curve in lace.

This method is used for either side.

### Simple Braid Lace

Make a pricking of pattern 30.

Wind 12 bobbins with No. 40 cotton.

The braid is made from six passives, 2 workers and the loop edge from four bobbins. The two workers connect the plaited loops to the braid, whilst the braids are joined by sewing-in with a crochet hook wherever they meet. There are three blind pins used at the curved loops in this pattern. For the cross in the centre of each trefoil, it is the best method to make three loops and only join them with the fourth.

*Pattern 30  Simple braid lace*

60

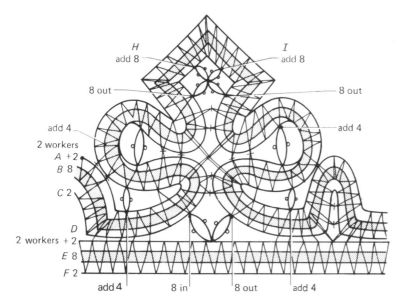

The following labels appear on the diagram:

H
add 8

I
add 8

8 out

8 out

add 4

add 4

2 workers

A +2

B 8

C 2

D

2 workers +2

E 8

F 2

add 4

8 in

8 out

add 4

*Pattern 31   Handsome lace edging*

## Handsome Lace Edging

Make a pricking of pattern 31.

Wind 28 bobbins with No. 20 cotton.

The braid is made of a pair of bobbins at each side, and eight passives in the middle. The pins are put in where the workers zig-zag across the braid.

It is better to work the straight braid edge at the same time as the pattern, in this way the 2 pairs of workers can meet and join up. For the crossed loops in the centre of pattern, it is better to work three and join them with the fourth. At G the outer pair of the inner curve is taken in as a passive and joins the braid again after the loop has been made.

To work the Catherine stitch join, it is necessary to add four bobbins and make a plait with a picot. Join it to the opposite braid, returning to where it started. Tie and cut off, leaving 3 in. of thread to darn in later.

The Catherine stitch, which is a plait with a picot, is often used in joining two braids, or to fill in large space, and must not be confused with a leaf shape.

At H and I, add eight bobbins at each of places marked on pattern 31. Make a whole stitch at centre and after making two more Catherine sts, tie and cut off the threads.

After a little practice and drawing the threads down occasionally, an even braid is made, even if it does turn and twist about.


## Collar Triangles

Make a pricking of pattern 32.

Wind 12 bobbins with No. 100 cotton.

The braid is made of a pair of bobbins at each side and six passives in the middle. The outer edge has pearls and loops are made on the plain side to which next braid is sewn in. Bobbins must be added to make Catherine stitches when they occur—and taken out when the stitch has been made.

It is better to work the plain edge braid as the pattern is joined as it progresses. It will, however, need another twelve bobbins for this.

In most Russian lace patterns, there are no pin dots indicated as pins are put in wherever necessary to make a close braid.

These Collar triangles are improved by thin starch before wearing.

62

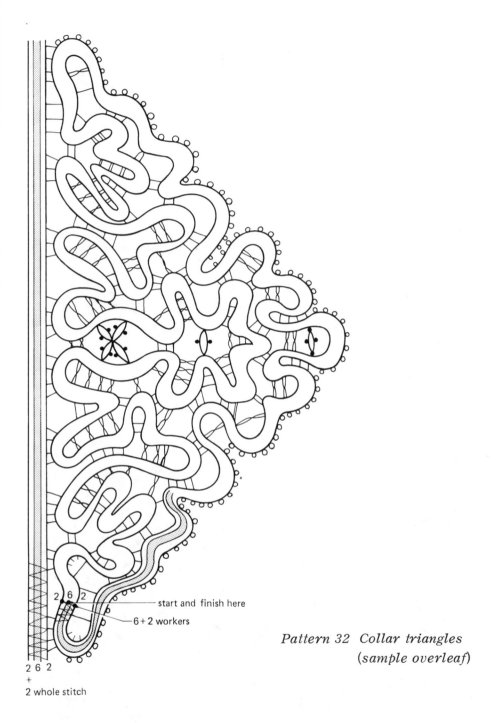

2 6 2 — start and finish here

6 + 2 workers

2 6 2
+
2 whole stitch

*Pattern 32 Collar triangles*
*(sample overleaf)*

# HONITON LACE

There is an old story told that the first Honiton lacemaker was instructed in the art by an Angel, who, in answer to a poor maiden's prayers for help for a marriage dowry, brought a pillow with all the accessories, and taught her how to make lace, thus enabling her to earn a dowry, and so to marry her true love.

Ladies of high degree, seeing the fairy-like fabric, were anxious to buy the lace. Having grown happy and rich herself, the fortunate young woman, in obedience to the Angel's command, taught the art to many poor girls, until the knowledge which was so wonderfully imparted was spread far and near.

Lace became an indispensable ornament in the dress of grand ladies, and the dainty craft became a blessing and livelihood to many of their poor sisters.

Fine lacemaking was introduced into England by Flemish refugees settling in Devon around the 12th century. The towns of Beer and Honiton became centres of the industry.

A town usually gave a name to a special kind of lace, so Honiton gave it's name to a particularly fine and delicate lace, which is still made to this day. It is made from very fine cotton, in small motifs joined together or mounted on net. The motifs are often in the form of flowers, leaves, butterflies, etc.

## Materials Required

A pillow as described on pages 7-9.
2 Cover cloths
Bobbins (at least 36 to begin with)
Fine cotton (No. 140)
Fine brass pins
Cotton, No. 36 or 40 for gimp.
Pricker, fine crochet hook, sharp pointed scissors, and a pricked pattern.

## Pricking a Pattern

Make a pricking, on fine card, from a pattern diagram.
Place this on pillow and fix with pins.
Fold cover cloths in half. Pin one over top edge of pattern and the other 1 in. below, leaving only a small portion of the pattern visible between the folds. After working the pattern the cloths are moved, thus keeping the lace clean.

## Pearl Point

For slender leaves, etc. this is better than a blunt end. To start a leaf, hang four bobbins at tip, twist each pair five times to the left, cross the twisted threads by bringing the left-hand pair under to the right and wind the four threads round the pin. Draw up tightly, thus making a Pearl.

## Plain Cloth Stitch Braid (with gimp)

Make a pricking from Pattern 33.
Wind 12 bobbins with fine cotton and one pair with gimp.
Place a pin at A and hang on two pairs of bobbins. At B hang one gimp and one fine; at C four fine, at D one fine and one gimp, at E two fine. Spread the bobbins out on the pillow. Start by making a whole stitch with four bobbins at A. Leave two and use the other two as workers. Twist three times, work a whole stitch through the gimp and fine thread at B, through the two pairs at C, through one fine and one gimp at D. Twist the workers three times, make a whole stitch with the end pair at E, put a pin up, and return with edge pair as workers, thus leaving a straight edge. Work across, always twisting three times before working edge stitch at each side. Work in this way until D.

## Gimp Braid

Using Pattern 33, work the edge pair. Now the gimps change places with each other, by slipping the right-hand gimp tail first, under other threads to the left, and the left-hand gimp to the right. Draw them together tightly, thus forming a cross on the under side of work. Repeat this cross at every tenth row, five times. Change the pattern at E.

## Pearl Edge Braid

This is worked as plain braid with a pearl worked at each edge using Pattern 33.
Starting from the left, work across until the right-hand gimp is passed. Then twist the workers once, make a whole stitch but do not put a pin up. Twist the workers seven times. Then with the right-hand, place a pin under the twisted threads, with a turn of the wrist, bring over in a loop, stick a pin in at E, pull the twist up closely and make a whole stitch. Twist the inner pair once and they will travel back. Twist the outer passive pair three times and leave.
Work across to the opposite edge and repeat.

66

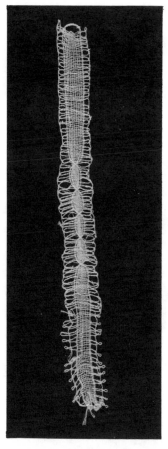

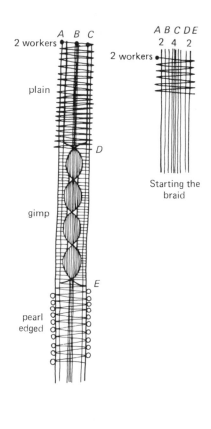

*Pattern 33  Honiton plain, simp and pearl edged braids—starting sequence on right*

When tightly made, these pearls do not untwist, but do not remove the pins until work is completed as this ensures a firm edge. Pearls and picots inside patterns are worked in the same way.

**To Finish Off Braids, Leaves and Stems**

1  Take the bobbins and divide into three portions; plait for $1/4$ in., tie tightly, to make secure and cut off.

2  Rope-sewing. Arrange bobbins in fan-shape, place right-hand pair to side, then pass outside a left-hand pair, over and under all the rest, several times to form a fine cord, finally tie the two threads tightly and cut off all threads.

67

## Whole Stitch Leaf

Make a pricking from Pattern 34. Wind 10 pairs of bobbins.
Hang two pairs at A and make a pearl point. Twist each pair three
times and put a pin between them at B. Hang eight pairs at B, and
arrange them on the pillow in a fan-shape. The bobbins now lie in
the following order, counting from left: one pair of workers twisted
three times; one pair untwisted; seven pairs passives; one pair of
twisted workers lying at the right-hand outside edge.

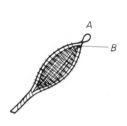

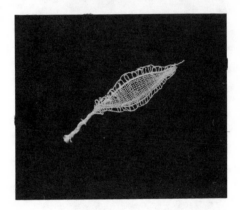

*Pattern 34   Honiton whole stitch leaf*

Take the pair of untwisted bobbins on the left and work in whole
stitch across, making seven whole stitches.
Twist the workers three times, make a whole stitch with the end
pair; put a pin up and leave two workers (twisted three times)
returning with previous workers, thus making straight edge.
Continue working to and fro, until within four pinholes of the end.
Cut out one pair in the centre, (tie one pair twice, lay the bobbins
back over the pillow to be cut off later).

Tie another pair in each of next three rows until six parts are left.
Make a rope-sewing for $\frac{1}{4}$ in., tie up and cut off the bobbins.

## Half Stitch Leaf

Make Pattern 35 and eight pairs of bobbins. Continue as for the
whole stitch leaf, working half stitch in the centre without cutting
out any bobbins.
*LARGER LEAVES* may be worked by the two methods with one half
in whole stitch and one half in half stitch, giving an attractive effect.

This method is often used for petals of large flowers. If the three leaves worked in whole stitch and three in half stitch are made into a flower, the centre may be a needlework buttonhole ring.
A student may be able to draw a simple design and work it in leaves and petals, so creating original work.

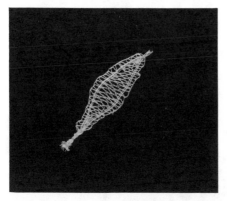 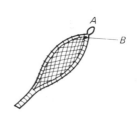

*Pattern 35   Honiton half stitch leaf*

**Whole Stitch Long Leaf** (with gimp)

Make pattern 36, and eight pairs of bobbins and one pair of gimps.

Hang two pairs at A and make a pearl point. Twist each pair three times to the left and put a pin at B between the pairs. Hang three pairs on B and one pair of gimps (on either side of passives). The inner pair of bobbins lying on the left of the first gimp is the working pair.

Work across in whole stitch until two threads remain.
Twist the workers three times, work a whole stitch, put a pin up, twist both pairs three times, leaving the right-hand pair, and return with other two as workers, thus making a plain edge.
Work ten rows, then put a pin at C and hang two more bobbins, allowing them to lie next to the gimp and drawing them down with the other passives.

Work two rows plain and add two more at D. Work two more rows and add two bobbins at E. Work straight to F at the left-hand side, when 2 bobbins are taken out.
Take the last pair of threads before the gimp, tie in a knot and lay the bobbins away to the right-hand side to be cut away later.
Take out a pair at G and H. Work to the last pin-hole, make a rope-sewing with the right-hand pair, tie off securely and cut off.

*Pattern 36  Honiton whole*
*stitch long leaf*

*Pattern 37  Honiton half*
*stitch long leaf*

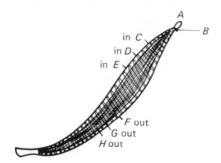

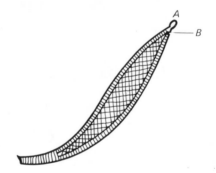

## Half Stitch Long Leaf

Make a pricking from the long leaf Pattern 37.
Wind six pairs of bobbins and one pair of gimps. Put a pin at A
and hang two pairs of bobbins to make a pearl point. Hang four
pairs of bobbins at B with gimps. The two bobbins to the left of
left-hand gimp are the workers.

The first two rows are made in whole stitch to make threads secure.
Cross each pair, right over left, to begin half stitch.

Make a plain edge at each side, twisting the workers three times. No extra bobbins are added in this leaf.

Arrange the half stitch carefully to become wider in the centre, and closer together at top and bottom.

Finish by plaiting or rope-sewing for $1/4$ in., tie and cut off.

### Whole and Half Stitch Rose Leaves

These are made exactly like the small leaves, starting at the tip of each leaf but a longer leaf stalk is made on the first leaf and the other two leaves are joined to the sides (Pattern 38). These are sewn-in. This is done by picking up a thread with a fine crochet hook, passing the second thread through it, and fastening off by tying and cutting off threads in turn, until all are joined in.

*Pattern 38   Honiton Rose leaf*

### Pattern with Curves and Fillings

Make a pricking of Pattern 39.

In making curves it will be found that the inner edge must be placed closer together than those at the outer, so a pin-hole must be omitted altogether.

Wind seven pairs of bobbins and one pair of gimps.

Hang two pairs at A, four pairs and one pair of gimps at B, and one pair at C.

Work a plain gimp braid, pearling the outer edge and plain inner edge.

Twist the returning workers three times, but the pair left behind are only twisted twice. On the inside of curves, one pin-hole is often used twice.

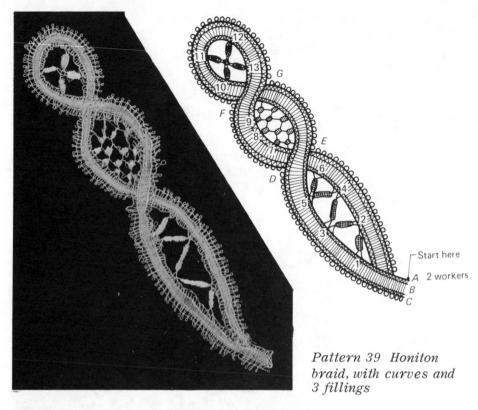

The braid has both sides plain from D to E and continues with
pearls on the left, and changing as it twists. At the crossings, the
braid is double. On ending, the braid is sewn into the side of the
first part.

There are three types of filling and these are included in Pattern 39.

*Cucumber*

At 1 sew, in two pairs of bobbins separately, make a whole stitch and
then weave a long bar. Make a whole stitch and sew pairs into the
braid at 2. Turn the pillow and repeat at 3, 4 and 5, finishing by
sewing-in at 6.

*Plaited*

At 7, 8 and 9, sew-in four bobbins. Make five plaited stitches. With
each of four threads, take two from the first plait, and two from the
second, to make the second row of filling. Sew two threads into
braid as soon as they are not required.

*Lead*

Sew four bobbins to braid at 10 and 11. Weave a small leaf with each, dividing the threads in the centre, crossing and making two more leaves, before sewing into braid where they are cut off.

## Motif

Make a pricking from Pattern 40.
Wind 12 pairs of fine cotton and a pair of gimps.
Starting at A, work in whole stitch for the bottom two loops of pattern, crossing over braids at B. Make the right-hand upper loop and sew in at C. Join in again at D, and make left-hand loop, sewing-in at E. The next part of this pattern is the narrow band.
Join in eight pairs and two gimps at F, sewing-in at G.
For the third part of pattern, join in twelve pairs and two gimps at H, working alternate scallops in whole and half stitch with pearls on outer edge. Finish by sewing-in at I. Work fillings 1 and 2 in lead, and 3, 4, 5, and 6 in block or plaited.

*Pattern 40   Honiton motif*

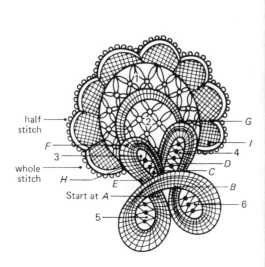
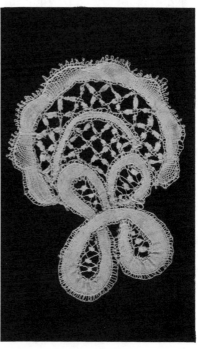

# Making Up and Mounting Lace

### HEM STITCHING LINEN

Measure the lace carefully and take a piece of linen the correct size, plus hems and turnings. Turn the edges of linen to the required size, make a hem, and tack into place. Draw out several threads from the linen under the hem. Cut a piece of linen from each corner to make a neat finish. (Fig. 7(a))

The threads pulled out of linen often may be used to make hems in coloured linen. You will therefore get the exact colour of thread to sew with. If these threads are not strong enough to sew, Sylko or Stranded Cotton of the exact colour must be used.

To commence hemstitching, run the thread under the hem from left to right. Make a small stitch on hem, now from left to right, slip needle under three or four threads of linen, return needle to left, and make a small stitch on hem. Take care not to sew through linen on right side. Continue to sew hem—be it a mat, tray cloth, or table-cloth—taking care at the corners and picking up the same amount of threads each time.

Press the prepared centre, and with small stitches, oversew the lace to the linen.

*Fig. 7(a)   Mounting lace on to linen by hem stitching*

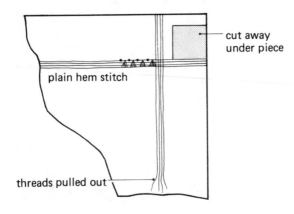

cut away
under piece

plain hem stitch

threads pulled out

74

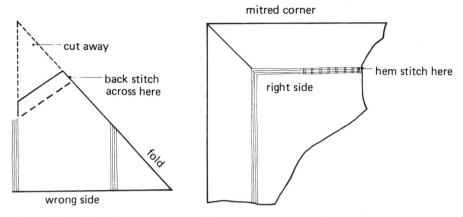

*Fig. 7(b)  Mitred corner mounting*

## PUNCH STITCH MOUNTING

### For scalloped or irregular edged lace

Measure a piece of lace allowing 1 in. extra all round for size of
linen. Mark even scallops on linen with a fine pencil line. Tack lace
to linen, $3/8$ in. from extreme edge. (Right-hand part of Pattern 41)

With suitable thread and fairly thick needle, work from right to left,
(see diagram). Start at 1 and make two backstitches on lace and
through linen 1 to 2. Now put the needle in at 2 and come out at 3
on linen only.

Make two backstitches 3 to 4. Put the needle in at 4 and out again
at 1. A backstitch is made from 1 to 3 and out at 5 on lace and
linen. Repeat this square stitch all along, pulling the stitches
tightly, thus making a mock hemstitch.

*Pattern 41  Button hole mounting (left) and punch stitch (right)*

Turn work to wrong side and cut linen away allowing $\frac{1}{4}$ in. which is rolled and oversewn to neaten back of work. Never leave raw edges which will fray and break away. Make this stitch finely for handkerchiefs and fine linen articles and rather larger for heavy lace and linen.

## BUTTON HOLE MOUNTING

This form of mounting lace to linen may be preferred. As shown on the left-hand part of Pattern 41, tack lace to linen very carefully and working from left to right, make very close button hole stitches over the lace edge and the linen. Cut away the surplus linen from the back but finish off any raw edges by whipping with fine thread.

## WHIPPING STITCH

Very fine lace may be whipped to fine linen, by oversewing edges very closely, following straight or curved lines (Pattern 42). Cut away the surplus linen from the back of the work and oversew this to neaten the edge, as in other methods of mounting.

*Pattern 42  The whipping stitch*

By following one of these methods, the article to be made is enhanced by the finishing touches. Great care must be taken to achieve good results.

# Lace Cleaning

### DRY-CLEANING

Old and valuable lace may be cleaned quite satisfactorily by the following method.
Lay the soiled lace on blue tissue paper, sprinkle powdered Magnesia freely on the soiled parts and wrap it in the paper. In a few days take the lace out and shake it until the magnesia is removed. If the lace is not quite clean, repeat the method again until the lace is to your satisfaction.

### WASHING

Sew a piece of clean white cloth over a long round bottle. Beginning with one end of the lace, tack to cloth carefully. Wrap round and round the bottle and secure the end by tacking carefully.
Be sure the lace is free from wrinkles.
Sew another cloth round bottle and lace.
Make a rich suds with warm water and any mild white soap. Soak the bottle and lace in the suds for an hour or two. Prepare more suds in a large pan and boil the bottle and lace for 20 minutes. If lace is not clean enough repeat the boiling again for another 20 minutes. Rinse the lace and bottle under the cold water tap, until all soapy water is gone. Place on a clean towel and pat gently until nearly dry. Now roll in another dry towel and leave until all the water has been removed. Take the bottle out of the towel and place in the sun to dry. Remove the outer cover and peel off the lace. It will look like new and need no ironing.

A piece of lace that is too large to be wound on a bottle must be cleaned in a different way.
Sew the lace wrong side up on a clean white cloth, large enough to take it flat. Sew all around the edge and across if the lace is wide. Soak and boil as directed above. When it is rinsed, shake the cloth gently to remove wrinkles in the lace.

Hang the cloth and lace in the fresh air to dry. Place on a thick ironing blanket, the wrong side up and instead of ironing with a hot iron, take the round smooth end of a bone crochet hook and run this over every leaf, petal, or other part of the pattern. This will smooth it out and yet will not pull it out of shape, as if it had been ironed.

## HOW TO STIFFEN LACE

When the washed lace is quite dry, dip it in a thin stiffening solution made up as follows.

Take some pure starch and divide it into two portions. Dissolve both in cold water. Thicken one portion by pouring on boiling water, stirring until cool, and then stir the cold portion into it. This will now be the consistency of milk.
Plunge the lace into this prepared starch and gently squeeze out without wringing. Then put lace on one hand and beat it for a few minutes with the other, to work in the starch. Repeat this process and then roll the lace tightly in a clean cloth, until you are ready to pin it out.

## HOW TO PIN OUT LACE

The bolster pillow is best for this, but a round, padded tin will do just as well.
Cover the cylinder with blue paper (which is less tiring for the eyesight) and take only as much lace out of the damp cloth as you can pin out at one time, keeping the rest covered up. Use pins fine enough to hold the lace without stretching it too much.
Lay the lace on the pad and pin the straight edge first, keeping a keen eye on the spacing of the pins. Place other pins in carefully, especially in the picots.
Leave the pinned-out lace until it is dry and proceed with the next portion to be pinned out. Slip each piece, as it is dried, into blue paper bag to keep it clean.

Lace cleaned and pinned out, needs no ironing and is restored to its original freshness.

## TINTING LACE

It is better to add colouring to the starch than to tint the lace at a later date.
Add a little strong coffee to make a cream coloured lace.

78

*Le Puy lace made from the pattern given in the 16th century lace-making pattern book. This book contained the first collection of lace patterns ever published and it is now in the Victoria and Albert Museum, London.*

Strong tea makes an attractive colour which is also very popular.

Other colours may be produced by cold-water dyes, if used sparingly at first.

### IRONING LACE WHEN MOUNTED

On a tablecloth or handkerchief, this must be done with a not too hot iron and when the linen is damp.
Iron the linen first and then push lace out carefully with point of iron, being gentle in order not to break the threads.

*A selection of traditional and antique bobbins—with their gold or silver bands, and brass-wired 'spangles'—alongside modern bobbins made from dowelling.*

# Lace Bobbins

Students seem to think that they need to be forever making more and more bobbins as they are required for the wider patterns, and that they need two or more pillows, say one for thick lace and another for fine work. It is very convenient to make a small pillow 14 × 10 in. on which to try new patterns, without having to disturb work in progress on the larger ones.

When the lacemaker becomes really keen on the craft and is on the lookout for bobbins, they will no doubt be found in antique shops. Before paying high prices for these antique bobbins, care must be taken to see that wooden ones are not affected by wood worm. This, with many bobbins put into one box, spreads quickly to others.

There are several interesting books on the romantic origin of some beautiful bone and ivory bobbins to be found. Please *use* any old bobbins you may buy, you will find them very smooth and pleasant to work with.

Fine East Midland types have names pricked out in red, green and black dots. Many bone and ivory bobbins have bands of pewter, called 'Tigers'; some have pewter spots, called 'Leopards'; some have brass wire twisted closely round the handles so that they resemble gold; many are very beautifully decorated.
A 'Mother and Babe' bobbin is much sought after, but difficult to find. The handle has a small baby carved inside and some have tiny bobbins inside. Once it was considered unlucky for a girl to use a Mother and Baby bobbin if she was not a mother herself.

It is a pity that so many people collect old bobbins as antiques and artificially increase their prices, whereas many a lacemaker would be happy to use them in the way they were intended to be used. Do *not* buy bobbins with broken heads, they are useless.

If antique bobbins are genuine, they have brass wire and hand-made glass beads as *Spangles*. I was recently shown a bobbin with a tiny book hanging at the bottom. It had a cover of Pinchbeck and inside were attractive pictures of Queen Victoria and Prince Albert, and two of the royal Princesses—a rare and valuable item indeed.

When bobbins have been cut off at the end of lace-making and they still contain a lot of thread, they may be joined together in pairs again, by a *Lacemaker's* or *Weaver's Knot*.

This is made by putting the right-hand thread behind the left-hand one, and over the left one, making a loop. Then, insert the right-hand short thread through the loop. Hold the old thread and a short end in the left hand, and the new thread and a short end in the right, pull tightly.
The short ends are cut off quite close to the knot, and it will be quite secure.

Wind thread on bobbin to hide knot, before starting a new piece of lace.

*Traditional and modern bobbins arranged on a sample of straight-edged Cluny lace. The famous 'Mother and Babe' bobbin is fourth from the right.*

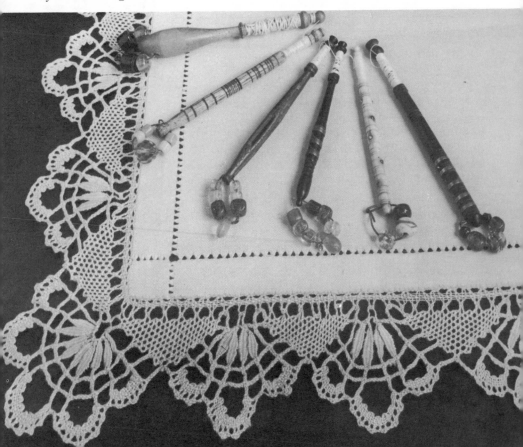

# Bibliography

## Modern Books

*Hand Made Bobbin Lace-work*  Margaret Maidment. Paul Minet, Chicheley. 1971.

*Pillow Lace: A Practical Hand-book*  E. Mincoff, and M. S. Marriage. Paul Minet, Chicheley. 1972.

*Pillow Lace in the East Midlands*  Charles Freeman. Luton Museum and Art Gallery. 1971.

*The Romance of the Lace Pillow*  T. Wright. Olney. 1924.

*Bobbin Lace*  Doreen Wright. Bell, London. 1969.

## Antiquarian books—possibly available from Libraries

*A History of Lace*  Mrs. B. Palliser. Jourdain and Dryden. 1902.

*The Art and Craft of Old Lace*  F. A. Von-Henneberg. London. 1931.

*Lace Making in England and Wales*  FitzRandolph and Hay. Oxford, 1927.

*A History of Hand-made Lace*  Mrs. F. N. Jackson. London and New York. 1900.

*Northampton, Bucks & Beds Lace-making*  A. S. Cole. 1892.

*Lace-making in the Midlands*  Channer and Roberts, London. 1900.

*Old Lace*  M. Jourdain. London 1908.

*Lace in the making—with Bobbins and Needle*  M. L. Brooke. 1923.

*The lace and Embroidery Collector*  R. E. Head. 1922.

*Devon Pillow Lace: History and How to Make It*  A. P. Moody. 1907.

*The Lace Book*  H. N. Moore. 1904.

*Point and pillow Lace*  Mary Sharpe. 1905.

# Collections of Lace

The Victoria and Albert Museum, London.

The Embroiderers' Guild, London.

The British Museum, London.

Waddesdon Manor, Aylesbury, Buckinghamshire.

Gawthorpe Hall, Paddiham, Lancashire.

The Castle Museum, York.

The Castle Museum, Nottingham.

The Museum and Art Gallery, Mardown Park, Luton.

The Roman Baths Museum, Bath.

The Royal Scottish Museum, Edinburgh.

*A display of lace by the author at a local craft exhibition.*

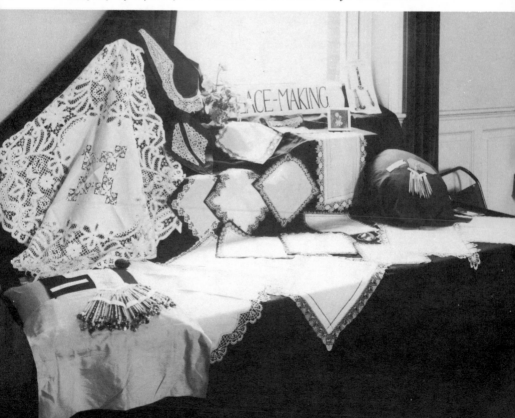

# An Encouragement

If students have worked carefully through this small book, I am sure that they will have obtained great pleasure from the results, and will have mastered an ancient and beautiful Craft.

Lacemaking is not the type of hobby that will earn you a fortune. Nevertheless, to make a beautiful tablecloth, first to enjoy, and then to hand down to a loved one, becomes a truly worthwhile activity.

Like many other handcraft teachers, it is my sincere wish that lacemaking will have a revival, and not die out entirely.

Ruskin said, 'The whole value of Lace as a possession depends on the fact of its having *beauty* which has been the reward of industry and attention. A really good piece of Lace, will show that the maker of it had fine fingers, and the wearer of it had worthiness and dignity enough to obtain what it is difficult to obtain.'

In conclusion, dear student, please enjoy your hobby, and be proud to say you are a *lacemaker*.

*Amy Dawson*

# Index